FIND YOUR MANTRA

A Journal to Inspire and Empower Your Life

ROCK
POINT
QUARTOKNOWS.COM
NEW YORK, NY

What is a Mantra?

In their traditional Buddhist and Hindu roots, mantras are phrases that are repeated during meditation or chanted in groups to bring awareness out of a person's physical body and into a higher spiritual plane. While there are many different cultures and practices that surround mantras, Vedic or Sanskrit mantras could possibly be the oldest, dating back at least 3000 CE. When these Vedic hymns are chanted, their unique vibrations and musicality are believed to make the chanter themselves vibrate with the special frequency of that hymn, and in doing so, they find deeper meaning outside of their translations.

You will not find Vedic chants in this journal, as the mantras included here are more modern and would not be considered a chant, per se, but more as pieces of a 6 7 formula for a fulfilling life. These mantras also come by many other names: prayers, hymns, mottos, cornerstones, catchphrases, and slogans, just to name a few.

Mantras like these are tools; when we indulge in destructive thoughts, as humans are known to do on occasion, we can build up a deeper negativity bias. By encouraging this negativity, we put a damper on the bright light that wants to grow within each of us. If we let our minds wander toward destructive thoughts, they will proliferate. Inviting positive mantras into your daily routines flexes the most optimistic parts of your brain. By changing the way you think, you'll change the way you feel. If you're feeling optimistic and opportunistic, you'll find that the road will rise up to meet you.

Mantras and meditations are tools for thought so that you can rebuild the way you think if the way you currently think isn't working for you. While you are learning how to wield these tools, be kind to yourself. Gently guide your thoughts to where you want them to be; retraining your mind will be slow at first, but with patience and repetition, you will surely pull through. These tools will help you construct your perfect "mind palace" and share your light with the people you cherish.

Mantras alone will not get you to your big goal, a greater spiritual connection to the universe, a fancy car, or love of your life, but they will put you in the right mindset to seek out that which will serve your best self. If your best self includes any of the things mentioned above, some form of them will come to you. Find love in your heart for yourself and love for just about everything else will follow.

How to Use This Journal

Find Your Mantra is a tool to help you transform your life through the power of positive affirmations that use meaningful words on which to meditate, inspire, and bring insight into your day-to-day life, thus empowering your dreams.

The following pages encourage you to reflect on how you experience peace, love, happiness, strength, and your individual journey. Each mantra is thoughtfully paired with powerful imagery and colors meant to evoke feelings of positivity and hope. After pondering the image and words, there will be a mantra action for you to perform. These inspirational instructions serve as calls to do a physical action to aide in body wellness, create a new positive habit to help you grow in spirit, or guide you to think deeper about the mantra you just read.

After engaging in the mantra action, you will be promoted to journal about your experience. These prompts serve as mere suggestions; you should interpret them however you feel is right for your specific situation. Know that these mantras and mantra actions can mean different things to you at different times. Depending on your current state of mind, the way you interpret a mantra today might not be the same when you come back to it in a day, week, month, or even years later. Be open to your evolution and embrace it lovingly.

If you're not sure which of the mantras sing to you just yet, do a bit of research about how others interpret mantras and see if empathy and warmth bloom within you. Perhaps you already know the type of energy you want to bring into your life but are unsure of the steps to

The dark is greedy, but you are bright. During meditations (or just when times are tough) flutter the eyelids closed. Elongate your neck and tilt your chin ever so slightly toward the sky. Find the sun in the dark. Everything will be alright.

How can you open your heart and allow in more light?

- Be kind with yourself
* pause & breathe
- patient
- stop resisting
- break compulsive patterns/behaviors
* Do one nice thing a day
- allow help!!

Good things today
- Saw pepper happy playing (felt present & connected)
- felt supported by Luz
- okay in accident - checked in/took accountability
- open to therapy/addressing anxiety
- felt more focused
- empathized w/ client

- I am lovable & worthy!

Gratitude.

On your birthday, make a list of people, experiences, feelings, relationships, and anything else you can think of that you are thankful for—as many as the age you're turning. Making this an annual, simple exercise will ensure that not a year goes by when you don't sit down and appreciate all the things in life that bring you joy.

Start your gratitude list here.

MIND

OVER

MATTER.

Changing your life comes from changing your thoughts. Set the pace for your new brain space. While you're falling asleep each night, imagine what the best possible version of yourself will do tomorrow. Reaffirm your worth in the mirror the following morning to set your mood for the day. Your life will be filled with all of the joy, delight, and fulfillment that you wish for yourself.

How are you going to put mind over matter?

NO REGRETS

Remove the word "mistake" from your vocabulary.
You no longer mess up; you only open yourself
up to opportunities for learning and growth. You
only participate in "happy accidents." Welcome the
wrong because from the foulest compost
comes the most beautiful flowers.

When was the suffering worth the "yes!" you committed to?

All I need is
within me.

Remember that whatever the circumstances are, all you need to get through is inside of you. There is nothing you cannot do if you only believe and act upon it. You're already complete, but don't be afraid to push the boundaries of your existence.

What new acts will bring more delight into your life?

An effective meditation for calming persistent fretting is to inhale the word "let" and exhale the word "go." It'll ease the current crop of concerns and calm new ones before they take root.

How will you give up being trapped and guarded and open your heart towards the future?

Peace.
Love.
Happiness.

Peace in your life comes from peace of mind. Find little ways to love yourself every day, so as not to lose the pieces of you that you cherish most. Happiness can be found in the most mundane places. Practice self-care, make more jokes, drink water, start each day with a made bed or a clean sink, go out, stay in, and do whatever little things make you smile, however bizarre, quirky, or normal they may seem.

How will you bring your core peace, love, and happiness to the people, places, and work around you that you treasure?

SMILE,
BREATHE,
AND
GO
SLOWLY

Leave an hour before you're expected somewhere and explore the area. Meditation occurs in quiet places where your brain has space to relax. Arrive in a space as your best self and enjoy this new experience with a fresh set of eyes.

What are the things you can do to go more slowly and see the world with fresh, calm eyes?

BE

THE

CHANGE.

Always remember to be the change that you wish to see in the world and in your life. Be something so entire and complete that you can't remember how gravity confined you to the ground for so long.

How will you embrace change?

Find a comfortable seat and settle in for a long
meditation. As time passes, begin to notice if parts
of your stance are uncomfortable. Do not adjust.
As your foot falls asleep or your elbow twitches,
sit in your discomfort and take deep breaths
until the feeling passes.

**How will you accept moments of discomfort
in order to grow as an individual?**

During your meditation, clench your hands into tight fists on the inhale. Clench your muscles. Shrug your shoulders toward your ears. Scrunch your face into pin-point features. Then on the exhale, relax it all. Roll your shoulders down your back. Open your chest. Release the tongue from the roof of your mouth. Unfurl your fingers and let whatever you're hung up on fall to the floor.

How will you commit to releasing tension in your body and your mind?

BE

STILL

AND

KNOW.

Take time to be still, look within, and listen. Allow things to happen in their own time. Stillness is the path to serenity. Be still, breathe, let go, and trust.

What bright moments can you draw from to guide you through dark times?

YOU GOT THIS.

Practice good posture. Stack the vertebrae of your spine on top of one another and hold your head high as if a string is pulling it towards the sun. Take a power pose, Wonder Woman-style, with your hands on your hips and your feet firmly planted hip distance apart. Let the channels of energy flow through you and don't dump into your joints.

Make an action plan to tackle whatever life throws at you.

Be
here,
now.

Ground yourself in the concrete truth of your body.
Take note of all the synapses in your body and explore
the feeling. Scan from the top of your head to the
tips of your toes, then go back up again to fully
ground yourself into your body once more.

Write about the times when your mind wants to be in one place but your heart needs to be in another?

Meditation is the sometimes tedious process
of bringing a playful and wandering mind back to
a place of stillness. This function of guiding your
thoughts to a quiet place will strengthen
your mind and ability to think.

In what ways will you create a more self-aware life?

Unblinking, effervescent, uplifting, and strong,
love wants to be shared. Love is infinite and it
yearns to be let out. Vent your love to all
that lives around you.

How do you practice love to truly be who you're meant to be?

Family is forever.

Talk to your family. Hear their voices. Connect to your past and let it be your present. Tell them often and loudly that you love them.

How can you strengthen the bonds between you and your family members?

I am.

Write it down and say it out loud. You are
who you say you are. "I am who I say I am."
By saying and writing down your affirmations,
you train your mind to believe them.

**Write down and then say aloud the things that
you want to be realized in your life.**

Choose love.

For every imperfection, complaint,
and gripe you have about yourself,
give yourself two compliments.

When your mind wanders towards unkindness, write down the things you love about yourself.

LOVE
AND
LIGHT.

Send love and light to those you think need it.
This can be a specific person or a group of people.
When you find a place of calm and quiet, send
good vibes to them, and a hope that their day is
just a touch lighter and more full of love than usual.

How do you plan to give as much love as possible?

NOT

ALONE.

Be brave, speak up, reach out, stay strong.
Never give up because it gets better.
Think positive and dwell on possibilities.

How will you benefit personally by seeing the good and never losing hope?

Follow
your
heart.

Intuition is a powerful tool at your disposal.
Guidance from your gut will not lead you astray.
Rather than rationalizing a less than desirable
choice, take the leap, listen to that little voice, and
trust that whatever decision you make is moving
you along toward your highest good.

**How will you follow your heart in order
to live your most authentic life?**

LIVE
WHAT
YOU
LOVE.

Do something every day that brings you joy.
Surround yourself with people who lift you up and
do the same in return. Choose a career that
allows you to do what you love.

How do you plan to attract more wellness and happiness into your life?

Take care of yourself.

Set aside time in your schedule for yourself. When life is busy and there's not a single moment in it that you can attribute to yourself, begin saying "no" more often. Practice saying "no" to excursions, and experience the joy of missing out so that you will be well rested and better prepared to take care of yourself.

Start your self-care to-do list here.

I
AM
WORTHY.

Decide what matters most to you in life, how you
want to live, the kind of relationship you want to
have, how you want to feel when you wake up—
make note of the big things and the small things.
Then decide that you are worthy of receiving these
things, believe in your heart that you deserve
the best, and work to engrave this into
your consciousness every day.

**List the reasons why you deserve goodness
and abundance in your life.**

DREAM
BIGGER.

Actively daydream about your perfect life.
Try not to think about material possessions,
but instead spend time charting out what the most
wonderful version of yourself would be spending
time on. What's the best possible outcome?
Don't be afraid to imagine your biggest
dream becoming a reality.

How will you achieve your big dreams?

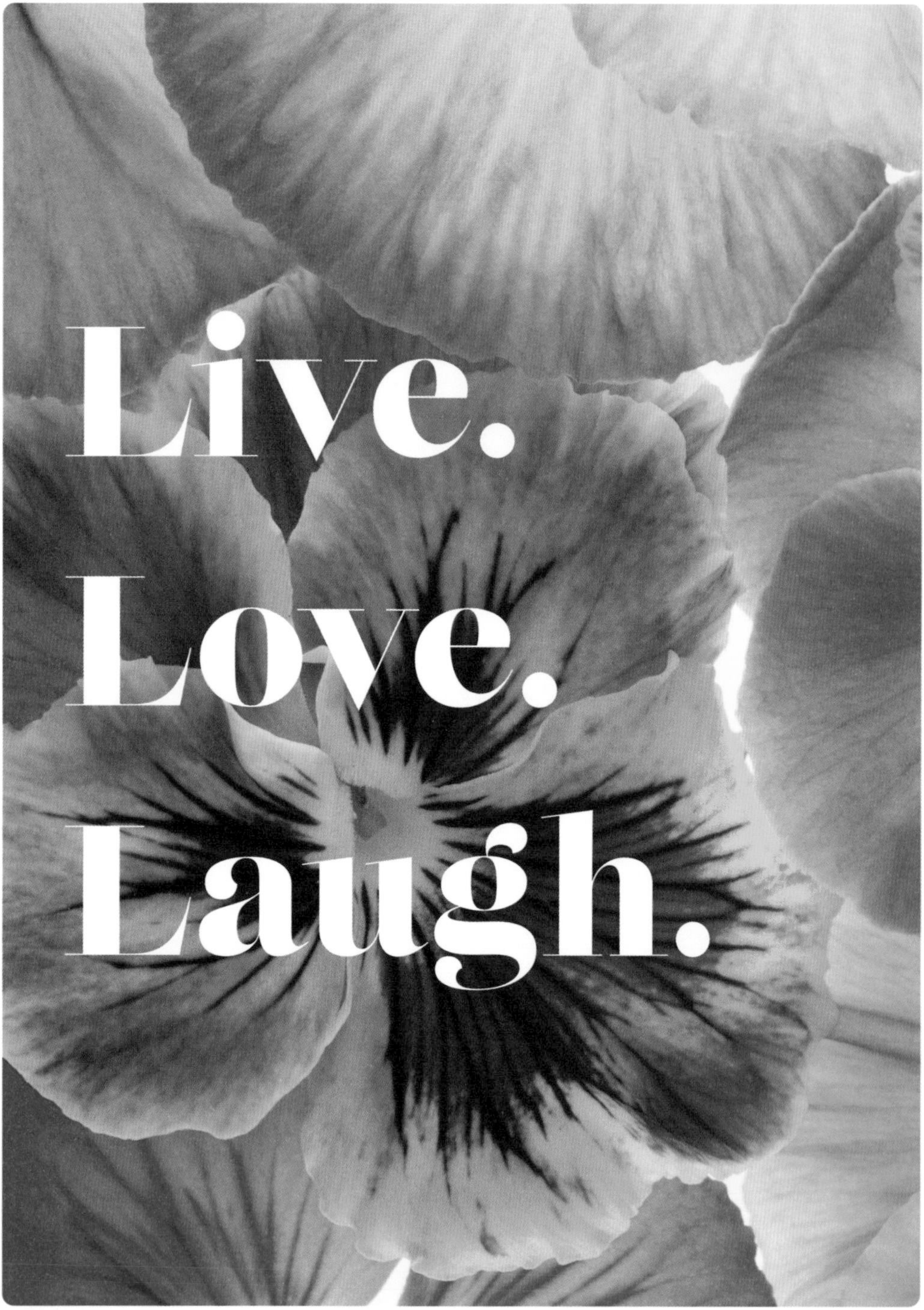
Live.
Love.
Laugh.

Observe your day. Are you present
and focused, or are you always multitasking?
Whether it's spending time with family or working
on a project, you will feel more fulfilled if you do
one thing at a time and are fully present in that
moment. Do you laugh often? If you don't, how
can you bring more laughter into your life? Love
yourself first, then love others unconditionally—
without expecting anything in return.

**How will you live intentionally, laugh often,
and love unconditionally?**

FOLLOW
YOUR
BLISS.

Bliss is a high-octane emotion that is not meant
to be felt in perpetuity. When you chase after it—
tailing it through obstacles—you're just an inch
away from catching its heels. Keep your eyes on
the prize, the fire churning in your heart,
and your feet on the ground.

List what makes you happy and plan when you'll give yourself a dose of these joyful moments.

On occasions when you can spare it, relinquish your choices to chance. You're luckier than you think, and this exercise will lead you to new experiences that will help you grow.

How will you prepare for opportunities so you'll be ready to take them?

Thought transformation is a process. On occasions where you find yourself slipping into less-than happy thoughts, try welcoming the opposite. "I am worthless" becomes "I am worthy," and "I cannot" morphs into "I can." When you start worrying about worst possible outcomes, shift your thoughts to think of the best possible outcome instead.

What negative thoughts do you want to transform? Rewrite them as positive actions.

BE
YOUR
OWN
KIND OF
BEAUTIFUL.

Accept yourself and be who you are. Relish
the fact that you are the only one of yourself.
See beauty in yourself and in others.

How will you inspire others to be themselves?

I am blessed.

At the beginning and end of each day, think of three
blessings in your life. Make this a daily habit.

**List everything that you consider to be
a blessing in your life.**

When plagued by feelings of insecurity or inadequacy, take time and really think about all of the little things you do in a day. Make a note of your goals and how you spent your time. Feel good about the things you did that you really enjoyed in the moment. Whatever you did, whatever you are, you are enough.

How will you celebrate the small victories in your life?

Expect miracles.

Manifestation is the practice of wishing and hoping for something so deeply that it comes into existence. First, to manifest a miracle, be clear on what you want. Have something specific in mind, and request it from the universe. Continue working hard on your goals. Believe in miracles.

Chart a path to manifesting your personal miracle.

BLOOM

WHERE

YOU

ARE

PLANTED.

Always strive to be your best self.
Stay positive, practice gratitude,
and bloom where you are planted.

**Make a list of the things you need to do to help
you grow in love and kindness.**

BE TRUE.
BE YOU.
BE KIND.

To be truly authentic we need to practice self-love
and self-awareness. Get to know yourself. While
you meditate, think about who you are as a person.
Kindly take stock of them and become
self-aware of the choices you make.

How will you ensure that you make progress on your journey to self-awareness?

Stay strong.

Every problem has a solution. Every lock
has a key. If you get knocked down, get back
up again. When you get frustrated with minor
or major catastrophes, take a deep breath,
center yourself, and stay strong.

**Write a list of encouragements you can return to
when you're barely able to be your normal thriving self.**

She belived she could so she did.

When you set a goal, believe in your heart
that you will accomplish it. When you believe
you can, you will be able to put in the hard
work and commitment to reach any
goal you set your mind to.

Make a list of goals that you want to achieve.

I'M A SURVIVOR.

When you are going through a rough patch
in life, remember your strength and know
that you will get through this.

**Write about the battles you have won and the
fears you have overcome.**

Born
Ready.

In the moment, if you feel the tingling of trepidation
or the brimming edge of doubt, center yourself.
Straighten your spine. Close your eyes and tell yourself,
"I'm not afraid to do this. I was born ready."

How do you prepare yourself to take on challenges?

Fearless.

Do one thing every day that scares you. It can be new foods, new blocks, new people, or speaking up instead of staying quiet. Try anything that doesn't come as effortlessly as breathing. Face one hiccup a day, and you'll be fearless in no time.

Write about a time you were scared but found the courage to power through.

THIS TOO SHALL PASS.

When meditating, picture bad thoughts like leaves or twigs on a lazy river. They enter your periphery for a time, then go away with little to no resistance. Do not chase them down the bank. Practice the art of letting go and embrace the fact that important thoughts will come back to you.

How do you move past hardships?

THOUGH
SHE
BE
BUT
LITTLE,
SHE
IS
FIERCE.

Know that your ability has nothing to do
with your size, your appearance, or your age.
Don't put limits on yourself.

**Reflect on a time when you were told that you
couldn't do something, but you persevered.**

Stand up for yourself, speak up, be bold, and
don't let anyone hold you down. Show kindness
at every opportunity you get because—a simple
kind gesture or a smile can make a big
impact on someone else's life.

When do you see yourself speaking and acting with a loving heart?

BE
BRAVE

In the face of opportunities and challenges, choose
to be strong and brave. Never be afraid of failure,
because failure is part of any success story.

Write about a time when you kept moving forward in spite of fear and challenges.

My story
is not over yet.

Everyone's life story has its ups and downs,
and so will yours. Whether you're experiencing the
lowest of the lows or you've conquered the highest
peak, know that this is just a chapter in your story.
Keep going, keep writing, keep living.
Your story is not over yet.

How are you making an impact on the world each day?

Visualize what you want from life and meditate
on how you can get to that point. Chart your
journey step by step. Visualization is more than
wishing and hoping. It's setting forth a course
to your goals so that your brain can create a map
that makes reaching them inevitable.

When have your actions been as great as your dreams?

When you feel like you are ready to give up on a goal, perhaps because it's taking longer than you thought it would or it's more difficult than you were prepared for, think of the reason why you started in the first place. Most goals aren't accomplished—not because they are impossible—but because the person gives up too soon.

Reflect on the times when you felt like you were fighting uphill battles.

MAKE
TODAY
COUNT.

Aim to do something every day that makes
your life or someone else's life a little better. For
instance, compliment someone; it will brighten their
day and make you feel good, too.

When have you chosen to take the steps to make life better in every way?

Remember why you started.

Meditate on current projects. Think about what inspired you. If it is a person or place, visit them. Inspiration does not die once you've harvested it. Tap the well, light the match again, and carry on.

How have you reignited passion for projects when you felt the flame start to waver?

Keep moving forward.

If you are chained down by the past, try
removing the clutter from your life to make room
for new experiences. Get rid of anything that no
longer serves you. Look to the future
instead of clinging to the past.

**How will you let go of the past and keep
moving into your future?**

BELIEVE

Say "yes" to more and then the little voice in your
head trying to pull you down will have to listen.
Believe you can do it against all odds.
Influential people with a good moral
compass need to believe in themselves.

**Write about a time where you put aside the voice
that says, "no," and chose to listen to the
voice that says, "yes."**

Follow your heart and have courage to
choose your own path in life. Choosing your own
path is a true sign of vision and strength.

When have you strayed off the beaten path to make your own way?

I am the
master
of my
own fate.

You are the protagonist of your story. Choose your path, and the road will rise up to meet your brave soul. Know that you are in control of a lot and that when the world asks you to relinquish control there is either a lesson to be learned or an alternative route waiting to be uncovered.

How have you empowered yourself as the master of your fate?

You only get to live each day once. Seize that opportunity. When you have a goal or a big task to accomplish, break it down into daily steps, then take it one day at a time.

What are some ways you can teach yourself to live in the present?

DREAM.

BELIEVE.

ACHIEVE.

When you set a goal, imagine the best possible outcome.
Believe that it is possible and it is going to happen for
you. Then work hard, commit, and persist
until you reach your goal.

**Reflect on a time when your abilities and
dreams helped to push yourself through
difficult times and failures.**

DO

IT

ANYWAY.

Sometimes you have to do something when you are not ready just yet, or your ego doesn't want you to do it. But you know in your heart that the time is right and that it is the right thing to do. Whether it is forgiving someone or letting go of a relationship, show courage, be strong, and do it.

When have you let go of a closed door in order to open a new one?

Anything
is
possible.

Think of things that people thought were
impossible but that you still accomplished. Remind
yourself that little miracles happen every day,
and anything can happen with faith
and hard work. It is the truth.

How will you conquer the limitations placed upon you?

ONE

THING

AT A

TIME.

You don't need to do it all. Do one thing at a time
and do it well. Delegate what you can, whenever you can.
Do less, accomplish more.

How can you keep your tasks, your goals, and your life simple?

Make
it
happen.

Make the decision that you will be successful in whatever goal it is that you are setting for yourself. If you want to live a healthier life, decide that you can and will accomplish that by taking action every day to make it happen. Once you have made that decision, make a healthy choice every day. Success in anything is but a series of daily habits.

What will you do each day to ensure that you not only survive, but thrive?

This edition published in 2020 by Rock Point, an imprint of The Quarto Group, 142 West 36th Street, 4th Floor, New York, NY 10018, USA
T (212) 779-4972 F (212) 779-6058 www.QuartoKnows.com

Contains content originally published in 2019 as *Find Your Mantra* by Rock Point, an imprint of The Quarto Group, 142 West 36th Street, 4th Floor, New York, NY, 10018.

Rock Point titles are also available at discount for retail, wholesale, promotional and bulk purchase. For details, contact the Special Sales Manager by email at specialsales@quarto.com or by mail at The Quarto Group, Attn: Special Sales Manager, 100 Cummings Center Suite, 265D, Beverly, MA 01915, USA.

ISBN: 978-1-63106-753-2

2 4 6 8 10 9 7 5 3 1

Publisher: Rage Kindelsperger
Creative Director: Laura Drew
Managing Editor: Cara Donaldson
Cover Design: Cindy Samargia Laun
Page Design: Amy Harte
Page Layout: Kim Winscher

Printed in China

This journal provides general information on forming positive habits. However, it should not be relied upon as recommending or promoting any specific diagnosis or method of treatment for a particular condition, and it is not intended as a substitute for medical advice or for direct diagnosis and treatment of a medical condition by a qualified physician. Readers who have questions about a particular condition, possible treatments or that condition, or possible reactions from the condition or its treatment should consult a physician or other qualified healthcare professional. The author and publishers are in no way responsible for any actions or behaviors undertaken by the user of this journal.